Dear Reader,

Welcome to the 7 Acts of Leadership Workbook. Congratulations on your choice to learn more about yourself, leadership, and managing change.

These activities are designed to help you develop your leadership style. It's up to you to determine the pace at which you reflect on each activity. There are no "right answers." This is your leadership-development canvas, and the exercises in this workbook are designed to move your thinking forward about your leadership style. The 7 Acts Guide is provided as a quick reference and memory jogger.

If you want to know the story behind each of these seven acts, I encourage you to read my memoir, *Pack an Extra Pair of Underpants: Leadership Inside Out*. In it, I share the story of how the activities in this workbook changed my life. My memoir was written to encourage people who question their ability to achieve great things and to inspire you to be the best you can be, regardless of what you've been told. If you have the desire for change, you have the potential for leadership.

To learn more about the future of leadership in the digital age, join me for a fireside chat at www.michellepallas.com. Tell your story, share your insights, and help expand the network of leadership capability!

7 Acts of Leadership Workbook

A guide for leaders in the digital age

by

Michelle Pallas

Michelle Pallas, Inc.
www.michellepallas.com

James,
Enjoy the hard
work that comes
with this!,
Michelle

ISBN 978-0-9895255-0-3

1. The main category of the book – Business Leadership. 2. Another subject category – Self Help / Personal Growth / Success. 3. More categories – Careers, Entrepreneurism, Management, Professionalism, Mentor, Coach.

First Edition

Cover and logo designs: Bart Rinke
BartRinkeDesign@gmail.com
www.RinkeWebandDesign.com
Copy editor: David Mesrey
Author photo: Jennifer Dery JoNa
Photography

Contents

7 Acts

ACT 1: KNOW WHERE YOU'RE GOING
Visualizing and goal-setting enables realization of dreams.

Vision Statement & Goal-Setting

ACT 2: BROKER CAPABILITY
Designing a network of talent requires knowledge of people.

Character Plan, Network Map & Network Capability

ACT 3: CONNECT
Making connections depends on a clear vision and a believable story.

Communication Assessment

ACT 4: ROLE MODEL
Deliberately selecting and being a role model defines character.

Reputation Challenge

ACT 5: CARE
The key to leadership.

Show You Care

ACT 6: HAVE COURAGE
Acting without fear after thoughtful consideration.

Courage Plan

ACT 7: LIVE RIGHT
Choices made when no one's looking.

Lifestyle Assessment

7 Acts of Leadership Workbook

LEADERSHIP POTENTIAL

This workbook is a hands-on guide to improving your leadership ability.

The 7 Acts of Leadership model is a practical approach to learning that's designed to demystify the concept of leadership. This program provides actionable steps you can begin to take today. Your journey begins with an assessment of your leadership potential as a baseline before exploring development activities.

LEADERSHIP POTENTIAL ASSESSMENT

The objective of this activity is to uncover your current thinking about leadership behaviors. Do you know what you're capable of achieving? Have you considered your leadership potential?

The results of this activity will serve as your baseline from which to measure personal change.

Instructions:

1. Consider each behavior. This experience belongs to you; it's between you and your inner self. Only honesty will bring a new reality.
2. Mark the degree to which you demonstrate each behavior: frequently, sometimes, or never.
3. Validate your answers with a couple of trustworthy people. Consider that there may be gaps between your view of yourself and the views that others have of you.

LEADERSHIP POTENTIAL SELF-ASSESSMENT

Leadership Potential Self-Assessment				
	Behavior	Frequently	Sometimes	Never
1	I have a vision of my future.			
2	I spend my time wisely in pursuit of my goals.			
3	I surround myself with people I admire.			
4	I know the capabilities of members of my network.			
5	I communicate so that I will connect with people.			
6	I'm a role model.			
7	I have role models in my network.			
8	I'm proud of my reputation.			
9	I care about people.			
10	I have courage to take calculated risks.			
11	I take responsibility for who I am.			

What's Next?

If you've answered "never" to most or all of the behaviors listed here, fear not. There's still hope for your leadership potential. If you're reading this book, you're at the point of curiosity. If you're frequently practicing these behaviors, bravo!

Caution!

If this assessment inspires you to make changes, you should be careful not to take on too much at once. Change requires energy, deliberation, and focus. You should aim to create new behaviors one at a time. (Yes multi-taskers, I'm talking to you!) And if you choose to do nothing with the results of this self-assessment, that's okay, too. But do consider saving it. You might benefit from it at another time in your life.

7Acts

ACT 1: KNOW WHERE YOU'RE GOING

Visualizing and goal-setting enables realization of dreams.

Vision Statement
Goal-Setting

Look into your soul to find your vision.
State your goals with eloquent precision.

VISION STATEMENT

The objective of this activity is to capture your dreams by documenting your vision.

Instructions:

1. Write a description of your vision as an affirmation, as if it were already realized. Try to include work, home, and community aspects of your life.
2. Jot down adjectives describing you in your future state. This is how you want to be remembered, your legacy.

See example below. Complete your own Vision Statement on the worksheet provided on the next page.

Vision Statement Example

The vision of my future looks like:

I'm a well-respected family-law attorney at a midsize law firm near my family.

I want to be remembered as:

Trustworthy, Confident, Independent
A Competent Mediator

VISION STATEMENT WORKSHEET

Vision Statement
The vision of my future looks like: I want to be remembered as:

What's Next?

After completing the Vision Statement Worksheet, write at least one goal that moves you closer to realizing your dreams.

GOAL-SETTING

The objective of this activity is to define the plan that will help you realize your vision. Writing goals isn't easy. Well-written goals take time and refinement. So give yourself license to just jot something down, knowing it will change. You can refine it as you're introduced to new concepts. And be careful not to take on too much.

Instructions:

1. Write down a goal that relates to achieving some knowledge, skill, or behavior that results in credentials or experience you believe is necessary to achieving your vision.
2. Complete the "because" phrase so that it forces alignment with your vision. Ask yourself if accomplishing this goal will move you closer to your vision. If not, why are you spending time on it? Maybe your vision needs more work. Expect this to be an iterative process, going back and forth between vision and goals.
3. Create goals with realistic deadlines. Be specific enough so you know when they're completed.
4. Prioritize goals so you can make good decisions about how you spend your time.

Goals Example
I want: To achieve a law degree and pass the bar exam within the next four years. *Because:* I want to practice family law. *So that:*   I can make a positive difference in people's lives.
I want: To gain experience in mediation. *Because:* I want to become known as an expert in mediation. *So that:*   I can improve my chances of getting a job in family-practice law and build a reputation as a respected lawyer in my community.

GOAL-SETTING WORKSHEET

Goals
I want: Because: So that:
I want: Because: So that:
I want: Because: So that:

What's Next?

Have you considered the adjectives you jotted down in the Vision Statement activity? Those words can help you design a skills-development plan or simply keep you focused on the things that matter to you. Next, we'll take a closer look at your Character Plan before examining the potential of your network.

7 Acts

ACT 2: BROKER CAPABILITY

Designing a network of talent requires knowledge of people.

Character Plan
Network Map
Network Capability

Surround yourself with people you admire.
Your network will grow as you desire.

CHARACTER PLAN

The objective of this activity is to capture your desired "character" before considering the makeup of your network. Your Character Plan describes the characteristics you want to see in yourself. This is the person you need to be in order to achieve your goals and realize your dreams. Who you want to become is your personal choice.

Instructions:

1. Using the worksheet provided, make a list of five people you consider to be role models either now or at some time during your life.
    a. First consider people you personally know: family, teachers, managers, neighbors, and peers.
    b. Next, consider people you might not know personally: politicians, musicians, actors, athletes, community leaders, and newscasters, among others.
2. Write down the characteristics you admire in them and why.
3. Highlight the characteristics you see in yourself.
4. Circle the ones you want to develop. Consider adding these to your Vision Statement (*I want to be remembered as*).

CHARACTER PLAN WORKSHEET

My Role Models	Characteristics I Admire in Them and Why

What's Next?

Now that you have a picture of who you want to be, it's time to deliberately surround yourself with people who represent your desired character.

NETWORK MAP

The objective of this activity is to identify key influencers in your network and determine their current membership levels.

Instructions:

1. Work quickly.
2. Using the Network Map Worksheet provided, make a list of seven people in your network. Surely there are more people in your life, but the first few ones who come to mind are most likely the people who influence you.
3. Using the Network Membership Guide, indicate their membership level by placing a mark in the columns that apply. Some people may have membership in more than one category. For example, a family member might be both a Native and a Guide.

NETWORK MEMBERSHIP GUIDE

Natives: As natural members, these people are family. They're permanent. These residents of your network may be Guides, as well as Courage Coaches. However, it's also possible for even Native members to become Aliens when they don't have the right characteristics.

Guides: These are people intentionally selected to influence you. You know them well enough to understand their capabilities. You know exactly why they're in your network. They provide value to you, and you may even provide value to them. These residents of your network can become Courage Coaches. You have a trusting relationship.

Villagers: These are people you know as acquaintances. You don't have enough information to understand their capabilities, or you otherwise choose not to invite them as Guides into your inner circle. Your relationship is not a trusting one. You might tap into this group when looking for new Guides.

Aliens: This category is reserved for people who threaten to negatively affect you or who have a negative impact on your reputation. Circumstances drive you to alienate them.

NETWORK MAP WORKSHEET – CURRENT STATE

Name	Native	Guide	Villager	Alien

What's Next?

Using knowledge of your current membership, build a network that enables your success. Surround yourself with the resources you need to achieve your goals. Uncover gaps in capability.

NETWORK CAPABILITY

The objective of this activity is to design a future network.

Instructions:

1. Consider current members from the Network Map activity.
2. Bring forward only those people you want to be Guides in your future network.
3. Write the reason you value their influence. It might be a capability they have or a character trait.
4. Once your list is complete, review the results of your Vision Statement, Goal-Setting, and Character Plan activities.
5. Determine if there are any capabilities and characteristics missing and document them on rows with no name. These are your network gaps that need to be filled.
6. Develop a strategy to find the missing Guides. Consider Villagers and Natives and ask your Guides to connect you with people in their networks. Consider going outside of your network to uncover new possibilities.

NETWORK CAPABILITY WORKSHEET

Name of Guide	Capabilities and Characteristics I Value

What's Next?

Now that you know who you want in your network, consider the amount of time you'll spend building or maintaining these relationships. Schedule time with the people who are important to you.

7Acts

ACT 3: CONNECT

Making connections depends on a clear vision
and a believable story.

Communication Assessment

*Words make a difference
when changing thoughts.
Connecting with your audience
is a gift to be sought.*

COMMUNICATION ASSESSMENT

The objective of this activity is to assess your communication behaviors.

Instructions:

1. Consider each behavior.
2. Mark the degree to which you demonstrate each behavior: frequently, sometimes, or never.
3. Validate your answers with a couple of trustworthy people. Consider that there may be gaps between your view of yourself and the views others have of you.

COMMUNICATION SELF-ASSESSMENT

Communication Self-Assessment

	Behavior	Frequently	Sometimes	Never
1	I'm aware of how my communication preferences and social style differ from others'.			
2	I work to understand my audience's views before crafting a message.			
3	I consider the impact of my statements before communicating.			
4	I show respect for other views.			
5	I listen completely without judgment.			
6	I look for ways to introduce people in my network to each other.			
7	I know the aspirations and dreams of people important to me.			
8	I can be trusted to hold conversations in confidence.			
9	If it gets emotional, I take a break from the conversation.			
10	I deliberately communicate through my actions.			
11	I inspire others to act.			

What's Next?

Now that you understand that your behavior is a form of communicating, you should see the connection between your communication style and your reputation. As you learn to connect with people, you influence their thinking. People listen to what you say. They repeat your words. You become known for the messages you send as a result of your behavior. Next we examine your reputation.

7Acts

ACT 4: ROLE MODEL

Deliberately selecting and being a role model defines character.

Reputation Challenge

*Say and do what's right,
and your reputation will soar.
People believe the message sent by your
behavior.*

REPUTATION CHALLENGE

The objective of this activity is to validate your thinking as it relates to your reputation.

Instructions:

1. Select five people from different areas of your life (work, family, social).
2. Ask each person the questions below. Add your own questions if you like.
3. Use this activity to further develop relationships with people you trust. Provide these questions before the discussion to allow them the courtesy of reflection before responding.
4. During the meeting, remove distractions, ask for brutal honesty and listen carefully. Take notes. You don't need to agree; it's *their* perception.
5. Allow yourself time to reflect on the results; pay close attention to any gaps between your perception and theirs.
6. Return to reflect on your Vision Statement, Goal-Setting, and Character Plan.
7. When you're ready, write a goal relative to your reputation, even if you think it's already been achieved. It'll serve as an affirmation.

REPUTATION CHALLENGE QUESTIONNAIRE

Reputation Challenge

My Current Reputation (This is what I'm known for today)

1. What's the first thing you think of when you think of me?
2. Why would you seek my advice?
3. What do you consider my strengths?

My Potential (This is what others see as my path)

1. If I wasn't in my current job, what could you see me doing?
2. What makes me unique?
3. What leadership qualities do you see in me?

My Weaknesses (This is what others see as my development needs)

1. Where do you think I should focus my personal growth and development?
2. What books, articles, or references do you think I can benefit from?

What's Next?

Use this information to manage your reputation like a company manages its brand. Consider gaps in your perception and the views of others. Your opinion doesn't count when it comes to your reputation.

7 Acts of Leadership Workbook

7Acts

ACT 5: CARE

The key to leadership.

Show You Care

Share this emotion if you dare.
It costs nothing if you truly care.

SHOW YOU CARE

The objective of this activity is to assess the degree to which your actions show you care about yourself and others.

Instructions:

1. Consider each behavior.
2. Mark the degree to which you demonstrate each behavior: frequently, sometimes, or never.
3. Validate your answers with a couple of trustworthy people. Consider that there might be gaps between your view of yourself and the views others have of you.

SHOW YOU CARE SELF-ASSESSMENT

	Show You Care Self-Assessment			
	Behavior	Frequently	Sometimes	Never
1	I make time to spend with people important to me, including time with myself.			
2	I show I care without enabling destructive behaviors.			
3	I laugh at myself instead of getting angry.			
4	I listen with my ears, eyes, and heart.			
5	I reduce distractions so I can listen to people.			
6	I'm worthy of the trust of others.			
7	I'm in control of my thoughts (my self-speak).			
8	I'm polite, I have manners, and I show respect for everyone — not just the people I know.			
9	I acknowledge others (no one's invisible to me).			

What's Next?

Caring is the key to leadership. Be sincere. Do people really believe you care?

7Acts

ACT 6: HAVE COURAGE

Acting without fear after thoughtful consideration.

Courage Plan

Face your fears and take the lead.
With good judgment, you will succeed.

COURAGE PLAN

The purpose of this activity is to establish a plan for courageous behaviors.

Instructions:

1. Consider each action.
2. If the action is something you already do, write down the date you started the behavior.
3. If the action is something you want to do, set a start date.

Challenge your thinking about decision-making, risk-taking, and courage. This plan encourages you to take action by setting a date to begin tracking evidence of your courageous behavior. As you work your way through this list, consider recording your accomplishments in a "victory log."

COURAGE ACTION CHECKLIST

	Courage Action Checklist	
	Actions I Plan to Take	Date
1	I will take inventory of things that are holding me back from achieving my dreams (fears).	
2	I will share my fears with a Courage Coach.	
3	I will take responsibility for my actions.	
4	I will hold others accountable for their promises.	
5	I will take calculated risks.	
6	I will maintain standards of ethics and professional responsibility.	
7	I will be trustworthy.	
8	I will share my rationale with stakeholders when I make decisions.	
9	I will be a Courage Coach to someone I care about.	
10	I will stand up for what I believe in.	
11	I will live the 7 Acts of Leadership.	

What's Next?

The journey to leadership never ends. Developing leadership behaviors is an adventure that requires energy, deliberation, and growth. If it gets easy, it's time to learn something new.

7Acts

ACT 7: LIVE RIGHT

Choices made when no one's looking.

Lifestyle Assessment

*Leaders are driven
by a belief about what's right,
never letting values out of their sight.*

LIFESTYLE ASSESSMENT

The objective of this activity is to assess your lifestyle and the impact it has on your reputation and network.

Instructions:

1. Consider each behavior.
2. Mark the degree to which you demonstrate each behavior: frequently, sometimes, or never.
3. Validate your answers with a couple of trustworthy people. Consider that there might be gaps between your view of yourself and the views others have of you.

LIFESTYLE SELF-ASSESSMENT

	Lifestyle Self-Assessment			
	Behavior	Frequently	Sometimes	Never
1	I behave in a way that members of my network would expect of a leader.			
2	I clearly communicate my boundaries about things I know are wrong, even when it's difficult.			
3	I have tolerance for people's opinions, even when I don't agree with them.			
4	I serve the community.			
5	My thoughts are consistent with my character plan.			
6	My thoughts match my actions and vice versa.			
7	I face my fears.			
8	I seek help when I need help.			
9	I live the life of a leader at home and at work.			

What's Next?

Only *you* can change you. Return to the first activity, Leadership Potential, and consider your progress.

LEADERSHIP POTENTIAL REVISITED

The objective of this activity is to reflect on your learning.

Instructions:

1. Consider each behavior.
2. Mark the degree to which you demonstrate each behavior: frequently, sometimes, or never.
3. Validate your answers with a couple of trustworthy people. Consider that there might be gaps between your view of yourself and the views others have of you.

LEADERSHIP POTENTIAL SELF-ASSESSEMENT

	Leadership Potential Self-Assessment			
	Behavior	Frequently	Sometimes	Never
1	I have a vision of my future.			
2	I spend my time wisely in pursuit of my goals.			
3	I surround myself with people I admire.			
4	I know the capabilities of members of my network.			
5	I communicate so that I will connect with people.			
6	I'm a role model.			
7	I have role models in my network.			
8	I'm proud of my reputation.			
9	I care about people.			
10	I have courage to take calculated risks.			
11	I take responsibility for who I am.			

What's Next?

Consider the progress you've made in the short time you've been working on this development initiative — and celebrate it.

7 Acts of Leadership Workbook

GLOSSARY

<u>Courage Coach</u>: A person who has an interest in the well-being of another. The Courage Coach takes the time to understand the vision and goals of the individual. It's a trusted relationship; one that can be reciprocal. The primary role of this person is to listen, ask clarifying questions, and offer guidance when asked. This person is skilled in identifying the presence of unfounded fears.

<u>Goals:</u> An intention or purposeful statement that sets a target for accomplishment.

<u>Vision:</u> Using imagination to see or internalize a future state.

25252211R00031

Made in the USA
Middletown, DE
23 October 2015